This book
belongs to:

Christmas Coloring Stationary Kit

Write Your Christmas & Santa Letters

North Pole Coloring Book

Sandy Mahony
Mary Lou Brown

We have fun at
the North Pole!

Elves, we have a lot of toys to deliver this Christmas!

Well, have you been naughty or nice?

Let's get the tree decorated!

Child's
Christmas Eve Checklist:
- I tried to be very good this year.
- I promise to go to bed early.
- I kept my room nice & clean.
- I tried to be kind & helpful.

Here is a sample letter to Santa.

Dear Santa,

How is everyone at the North Pole? I am sure you and the elves have been busy! Thank you for the gifts from last year. I have been really good this year! I have three things on my Christmas list: Grandma & Me coloring books, a visit from my grandparents during the holidays, and some warm boots for winter.

Thank you!

P.S. I promise to be asleep when you come down the chimney!

It's almost Christmas!

Reindeer, get the sleigh ready!

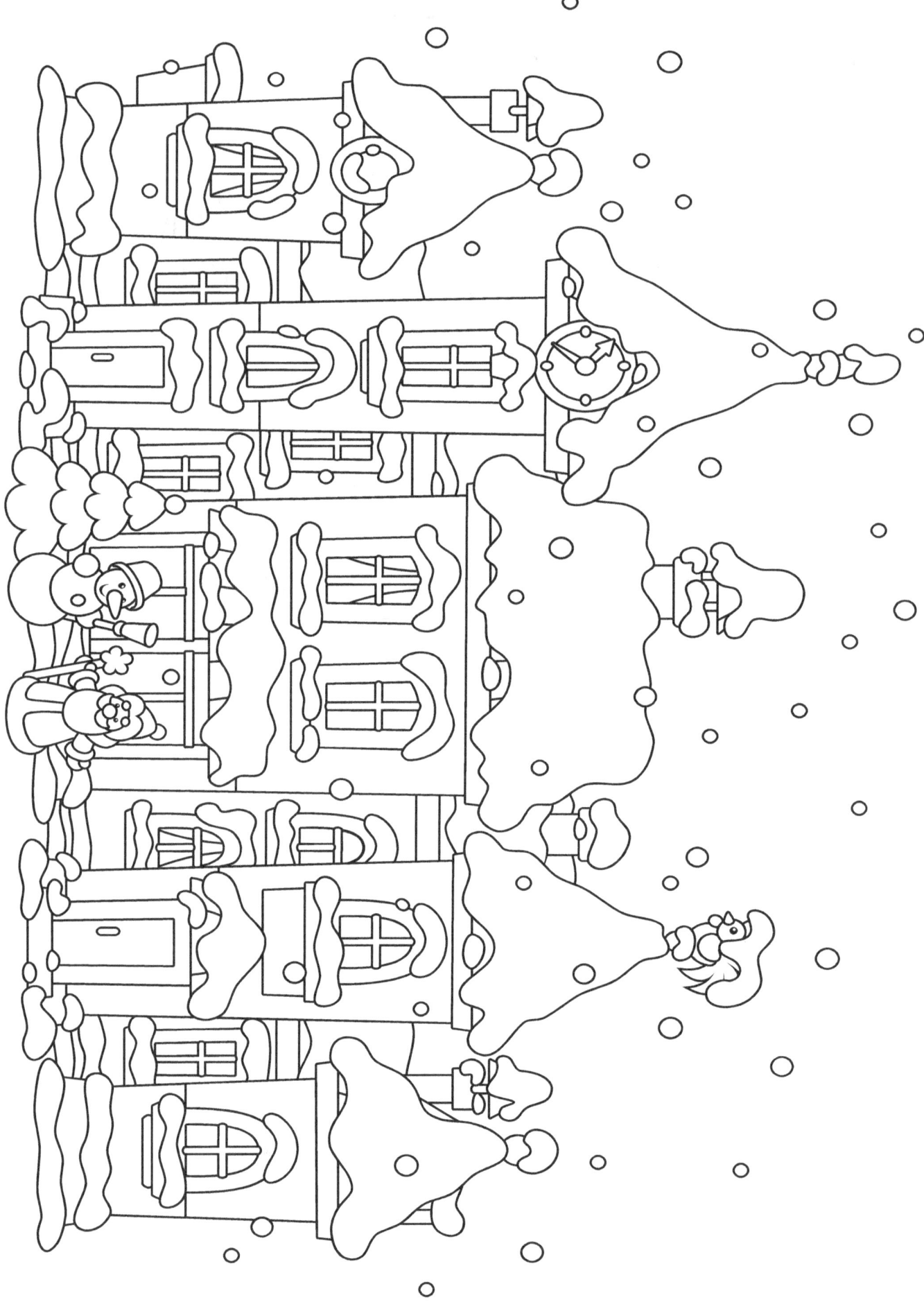

The North Pole

Dear Friend,
My elves told me you've been very good this year! I'm proud of you! We've been busy at the North Pole. Remember, the best part of Christmas is spending time with family & friends. I hope you enjoy your gifts. Have a wonderful Christmas!
Santa Claus

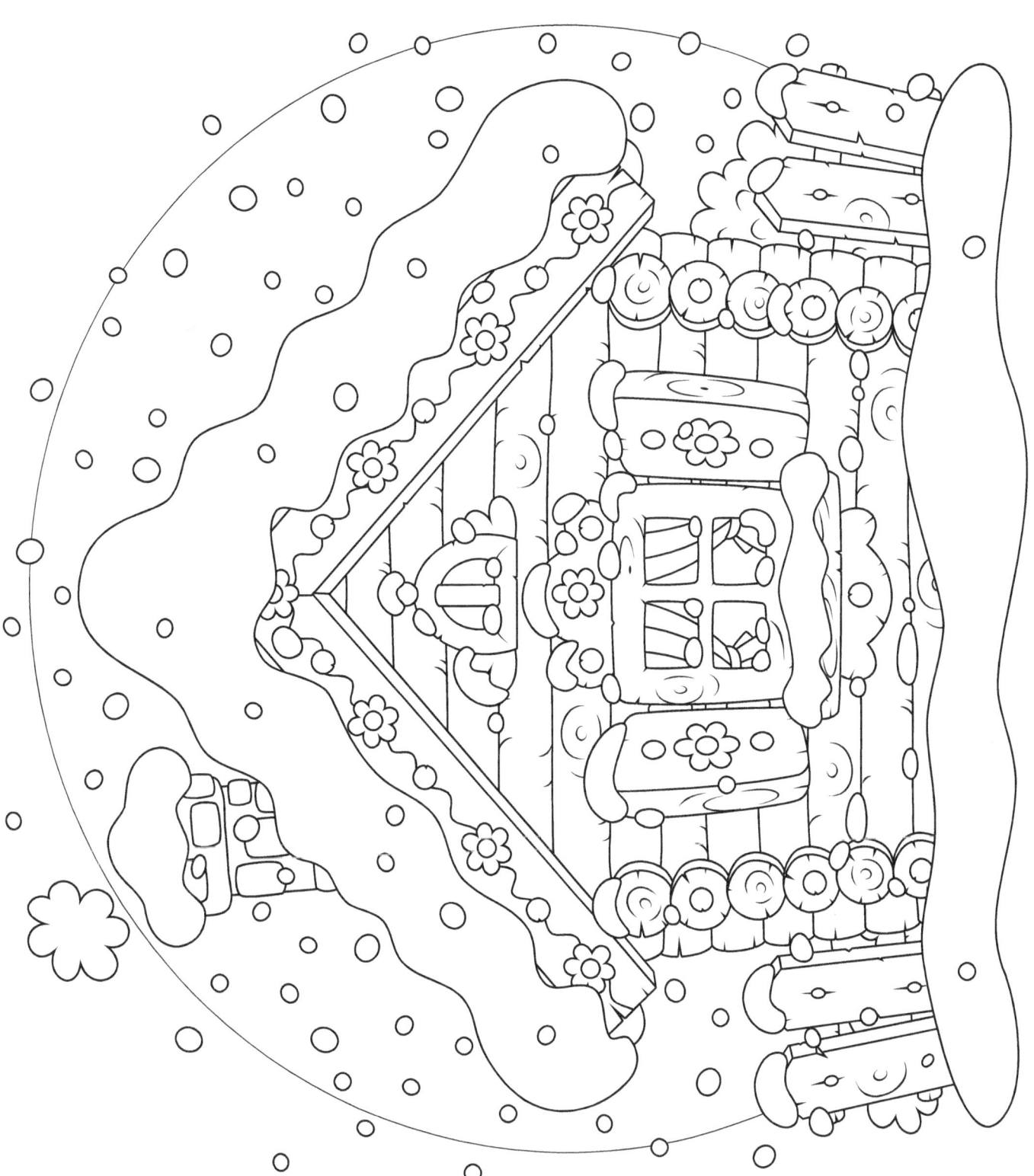

Dear Santa Claus,

We hope you enjoy the milk and cookies! Please give the carrots to the reindeer.

Merry Christmas!

I think I'll start my journey here!

Color the following Christmas stationary pages.

Remove From Book & Use For...

- Santa letters & notes
- Christmas letters & notes
- Thank you notes
- Drawings
- Lists
- Recipes
- Your ideas!

MAIL

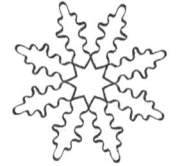

Merry Christmas!

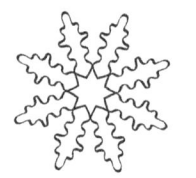

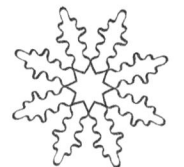

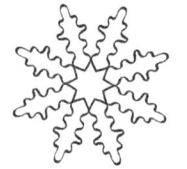

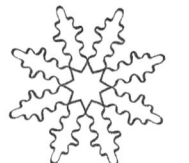

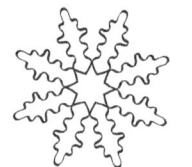

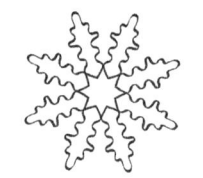

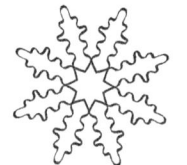

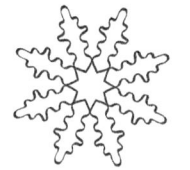

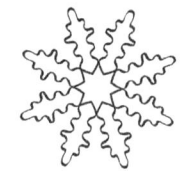

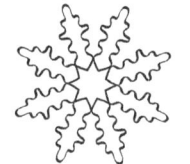